Spring 2015

Volume 3 Issue 1

Editor—Nichole Hansen

Editor—Tevin Hansen

Cover Art—Denny Marshall

Stinkwaves Magazine

www.stinkwavesmagazine.com

"Because adults don't give out
Stinkwaves . . . only children do that."

—Roald Dahl, *The Witches*

Stinkwaves Magazine Spring 2015

Handersen Publishing

WHaT'S INSiDe

WHaT'S INSiDe CoNt.

Featured Artists in this Issue

"I came to play."

Play – Jay Duret

From the Storyteller Guy

Hello all! It's been a while, but now we're back. Hard to believe, but it has been a whole six months since the last issue of *Stinkwaves* was released…back in October 2014.

We are now coming to you live from…*dah-dah-dah-dah-daaaa*…Lincoln, Nebraska! We decided to pull the plug on beautiful Northern Idaho (Coeur d'Alene) and relocate in order to be closer to family. My wife, who is from the Midwest (Kansas) initially thought I was joking when I told her we might be moving to Nebraska in the very near future.

The first rumblings of my idea to move came about right after the Halloween issue of *Stinkwaves*. The running joke is that now— after 4 months of living here—I still occasionally ask: "Do you still think I'm joking?"

What cinched the deal was something that both of us had given up hope on ever having again: a life. Then I uttered that one word that all parents know is the quintessential, most beautiful, and usually most unattainable word in all of the English language—at least for those parents who have absolutely no family where they live.

"Babysitters," I said.

That was all it took for her to become sold on the idea. Grandma and Grandpa would be 3 hours away! That would mean more time to write, edit, and format, all without two little ones wanting to "show you" something or crying "Up! Lap, *pw-ease!*" the moment (the very second!) you sit down at the computer.

We rolled out of town on December 5th 2014.

As for the 1400 miles between Idaho and Nebraska, I personally, had a wonderful, peaceful, relaxing drive, rocking out to some Pandora and checking out the scenery. I was driving the U-Haul . . . alone. To find out what life was like in the minivan with two toddlers, you'll have to ask my wife, but I wouldn't suggest it. The weather could not have been better—especially considering that I up and quit my job (2 jobs, actually) in the middle of winter.

The first three hours were miserable, and intense, and the snow kept things interesting. Once we passed Missoula, Montana, however...looking out the window you would've thought it was summertime.

It took some time to get settled, but now Handersen Publishing is back in the groove. Our original plan was to help other writers, poets, and illustrators find a home for their work.

That is still the goal. So with that being said...

Enjoy the issue!

The Storyteller Guy

Looking for Stinkwaves

Colin W. Campbell

Want a stinkwave, one or two?

For a stinkwave, use Yahoo.

For more stinkwaves

Google saves

stinkwaves (and stinky stuff too).

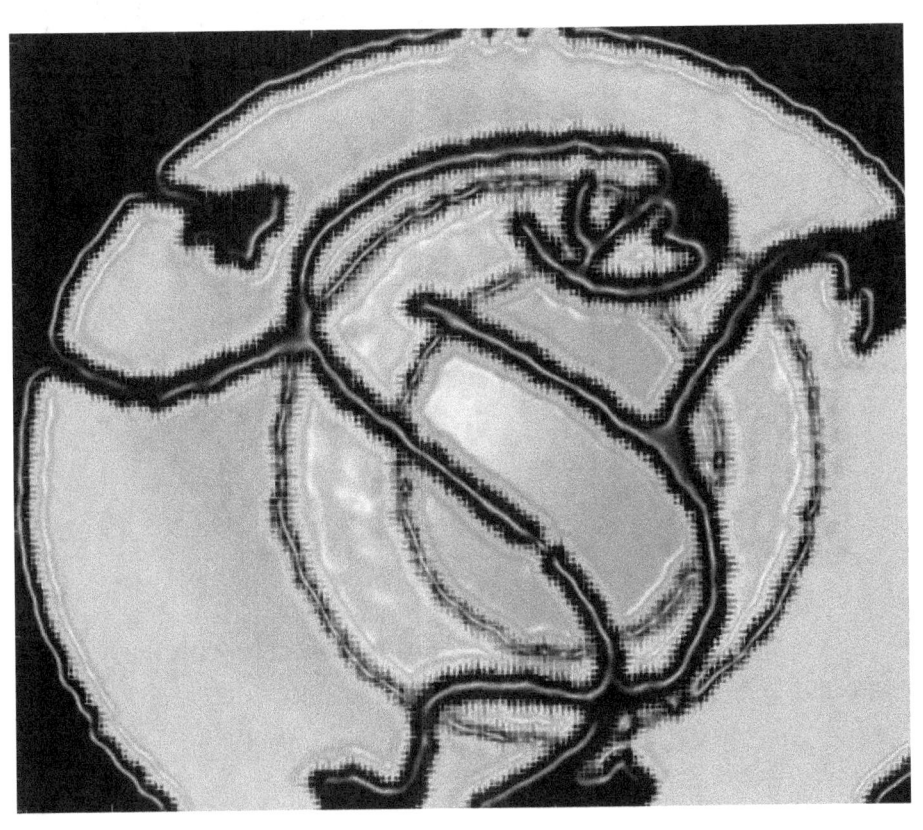

Peanut Shuffle - Kyle Hemmings

The Black Box

By Laurie Meyers

"Give me that piece of chocolate!" I yell, chasing Jayden around the corner. He screeches to a halt, but I can't stop in time. My cheek and shoulder crash into a board.

"Oh yeah, Makayla," Jayden says, "you should slow down because the kitchen appears to be closed off."

"Thanks a lot for the warning," I reply and rub my face. He splits the morsel in half and hands me the peace offering. The sweetness fills my mouth as concern clouds my mind.

"Let's get out of here," I say.

"Seriously, Mom should've told us she was remodeling again," he says.

"Maybe she's tired of you eating everything in sight," I tease. Jayden drops scraps as we walk, but I ignore it.

"Jayden, there you are," Dad says. "Hey, um, we noticed the food stash was missing."

"So what?" Jayden says.

"We were wondering if you had, well, eaten it."

"Like eaten *all* of our food?" he says. "You guys are crazy!" Sure, my brother is a food vacuum, but even his appetite isn't that big.

"Is that why you closed off the kitchen?" I ask.

"What do you mean?" Mom asks. "You couldn't get into the kitchen?"

"You should've seen Makayla slam into the barrier," Jayden says a little too happily. I shoot him a look.

"That's strange," Dad says. He paces across the room. "What are those barbarians up to now?"

"Look at the mess on your face," Mom says nervously wiping my cheeks. "Have you been leaving crumbs around the house?"

"Not me," I say truthfully, but I glance at Jayden.

Dad turns back to us. "Please be careful you two."

In bed, my brain churns with worry about the kitchen barricade and the missing food. My parents always scrounge for food for us. I wonder what they will find us to eat tomorrow.

"Jayden?" I whisper. "Are you awake?" I sit up. His bed is empty.

I creep into my parents' room. I'm stunned to find my big brother curled up in their bed. I wiggle in between Mom and Jayden and let my breathing slow to their drowsy rhythm.

The smell of food wakes me in the morning. I shake Jayden, and we race toward the scent. Instead of breakfast, a black box fills the hallway. Irresistible odors radiate from the box. We scamper toward Mom and Dad who are examining the smooth black sides.

"Guys, please, go back to your room," Mom says.

"We didn't do anything!" Jayden yells.

"We want to see what it is," I say.

"Now," Dad adds in his no-negotiation voice.

I tug Jayden, and he drags his feet behind me. My tummy rumbles with hunger and guilt. We are being punished for leaving a mess yesterday; I'm sure of it. Jayden mutters angrily next to me.

"What do you think is in that box?" I ask.

"Probably the biggest smorgasbord ever. Mom and Dad are hiding the food since apparently I eat too much," Jayden spits out.

"They wouldn't do that."

"Whatever. I'm going to check it out."

"Do you think it's safe?"

"Mom and Dad are overprotective. Like that story they always tell about Uncle Ralph stepping on the trap and..." Jayden doesn't need to finish. I remember how the story ends.

We wait an hour. Mom sets about cleaning feverishly, like someone with something to hide. We sneak out of our room and hustle down the hallway. Jayden sticks out his foot, tripping me and sending me rolling toward the box.

"You should be more careful, fuzzface," he taunts.

"Nice. Could you please take this seriously?"

"Whatever, you'll be calling me a hero when I come out with handfuls of food." Without a moment's hesitation, Jayden walks into the box.

"What's in there?" I whisper and listen hard for an answer. "Quit messing with me, Jayden. Come back out."

When he doesn't come out, I crawl around the box. There are no other openings. I push my ear against the box, but I can't hear any movement. I hold my hand in the air, wanting to knock on the box, but fear paralyzes my fingers. We get into trouble all the time, but this is more serious.

"What am I going to tell Mom?" I sigh. My cheek twitches. My parents are standing across from me.

"Makayla, where's Jayden?" Dad asks calmly.

"We were just...He, um," I stammer. Heat runs over my face. "He's in the box."

Mom lunges toward the box, but Dad stops her.

"Get your paws off me!" she yells and runs away. I watch Dad's face go blank. I know what he fears. Jayden is dead.

I spend the day replaying the events. Ethan walking into the box with a smug smile. Dad leaning against the box with his eyes closed. Mom sobbing in her room. I lie in Jayden's bed, breathing in his scent. My eyes are glued to the door, ready for him to walk in and call me fuzzface. I hear a voice in the hall, but it isn't Jayden's.

"I need to know if he's really gone," Mom says.

"Honey, I'll search the box. I won't stop until I find him," Dad says. "Jayden's always getting himself into and out of jams.

Literally. Remember when he got stuck in the jelly jar?" He lets out a soft laugh as they go to bed.

Dad's attempt to make Mom feel better makes my heart sink. If there is a chance, they would be doing something right *now*. Even though my stinking brother drives me crazy, I can't go on without him. I need to know, too.

I scurry out of my room and down the hall. The box appears before I'm ready. The black structure looms larger than I remember. The smell of cheese wafts under my nose, more pungent than before.

I take a few tip toe steps up the ramp to the small opening, not quite committed to the task. I pause at the top, sucking in the darkness in front of me. My next step falls through the air. I tumble to the bottom.

"Makayla! I knew you would come," Jayden calls. "You're so stupid."

"And you're okay!" I say ignoring his joke.

"Yeah, I'm alright. But now you're stuck. There's no way out."

I scratch at each corner and try to climb the wall. He's right. There's no escape. My stomach aches from a long day without food. I eat a little of the cheese, though the thought of it being a deception makes my stomach turn.

Suddenly, the box starts moving. We huddle together as our prison bobs along. When it stops, I brace myself. I know what traps do. Instead, a sliver of light appears. After my eyes adjust, I see grass.

"Freedom," I whisper.

"Not yet," Jayden says. "On the count of three, run."

I dig in my claws and brace for a sprint.

"One. Two." We both shoot across the grass and dive under a log.

"Three," Jayden says as I pull a leaf over our heads.

"We're on our own now," I say between gasps of fresh air.

"What about Mom and Dad?" Jayden asks.

"They're too careful to get caught," I say. "Still, I hope they keep using this mousetrap and not the Uncle Ralph kind."

THE BOOK

By Lela Marie De La Garza

Alicia turned the final page and put the book down with a feeling of disappointment. Frances Garner was one of her favorite authors, and she'd expected more from "Eastern Moon." Just then Prince, her Burmese cat, came into the room and jumped up beside his mistress. He saw "Eastern Moon" lying on the table and asked, "Good book?"

Alicia wrinkled her nose. "Not really. I like Frances Garner's work, and I was really enjoying this book till she brought in the talking dog. That was too much."

Prince laughed. "Ridiculous! Everyone knows dogs can't talk. Writing a book about one is like writing a book about a stupid cat. There's no such thing. Now, have you seen the paper anywhere around? I want to finish reading an article about power naps."

The Hour - Denny Marshall

CHERRY EYES

By Monica Adrian

Two pancakes embellished with decorative smiley-faces made their way hastily from the kitchen in the careful hands of a youthful waitress onto the table of yet another customer. Pete's Diner, located in the town mall, had the unequivocal high pulse of a place booming with business. The sounds of whining kids and clinking plates condensed into an oppressive clamor making it difficult for the waitress to concentrate. She discreetly wiped the sweat from her brow after delivering the order of cheerful pancakes.

The customer who had ordered the meal was of no more than ten years of age. The waitress found it odd that she should be alone. Just as she was about to turn away, the little girl impudently grabbed a hold of the bottom of her apron to direct her to turn back toward her.

The young girl showily looked at her plate with repugnance.

"Is something the matter?" the waitress asked cordially.

"Yes, something is the matter." She pointed a thick accusing finger at her plate. "Why did you give me a plate of evil pancakes?"

The waitress stood there confused, wondering if she was playing some sort of childish joke on her. As she waited for the appropriate words to say back, she stared transfixed on the downward slope of the young girl's caterpillar eyebrows.

The girl squinted her eyes, making her fierce eyebrows twitch as she noted the waitress's name tag. "Shelby!" The name resounded from her bulbous lips. "I asked you a question. Why did you give me a plate of evil pancakes?"

Shelby had no idea what to do, but continued to stare at the formidable eyebrows in horror. She couldn't quite comprehend that someone with such an adorable age as ten could be, though she hated to say it, ugly.

"Look at these Pancakes!"

Shelby looked down at the breakfast plate of two pancakes with maraschino cherries for eyes and a flimsy strip of bacon for the smile. "I see nothing wrong with them, miss."

"The eyes are red. The eyes are evil!" she exclaimed robustly.

"They are just cherries sweetie." The waitress, however bewildered, needed to get back to her other customers where she'd be tipped far better.

"I don't care! They are red and I won't eat them! And I'm not your sweetie! My name is Lucy!"

Submitting to the girl's outlandish rationale, for she was beginning to make a scene, Shelby took the plate and offered, "Why don't I just take your pancakes and fix them in the kitchen." Lucy impishly smiled at her departure.

After thoroughly wiping off the cherries, Shelby scavenged for the proper substitute. She opened up the massive refrigerator with effort. After weighing out carrots, peas, and tater tots, she nestled on some blueberries to exchange them with. She then quickly made her way back out into the commodious diner.

She searched and searched but the table could not be found. Then she realized that the table was there, only that little Lucy was now absent.

Shelby, not quite knowing what to do, rested the plate on the table anyway and asked the manager if he had seen her.

"I didn't see any little girl come here alone," Todd told her.

"Are you sure?"

"I'm sure," Todd confirmed. "Either way, our hostesses are not allowed to admit anyone so young to come here unaccompanied by an adult."

"Well, I was serving this little girl, and well, I guess she's not here anymore," she answered despairingly. Without another word, the waiter had already taken off with his duties.

At that, Shelby turned to the hostess to ask her about such a girl, but again such a girl there was not.

She suddenly felt that she had been foolish in taking a child's orders seriously. Shelby, after refilling several glasses of water along the way, went back to the table to clear her plate.

When she took the plate in her hands again at the sight of the pancakes she became so startled she dropped it and it shattered onto the tiled floor. The eyes were red again. She remembered distinctly that she replaced them for blueberries, but instead she saw the same ominous cherries glowering at her. At the sound of the plates crashing, like a thunderous explosion, all eyes in the diner turned to stare at her with such intensity Shelby envisioned them to be eyes of the same sinister crimson color.

"The eyes are evil! The eyes are evil!" Shelby cried out hysterically. She became dizzy as the whole diner swirled into a gyration of colors. A cold sweat suffused itself on her skin, and finally she fainted to the ground.

***

Plates were plummeting from the heavens. No, was it the heavens or was she in hell? Yes, she was in hell, and the plates were coming from a fiery stratosphere like a dome engulfing her. The plates like bombs continued to shatter onto the street. She looked around the dilapidated buildings. She saw Abercrombie, Hollister, American Eagle, Zumiez, all half-erect with their signs hardly visible through the destruction. Flames were engulfing everything. The plates hit the rooftops, creating new fiery combustions. She was in the Town Mall, but at its current state it was almost unrecognizable. Suddenly a plate came vaulting for her head which she dodged just in time. The bare street where it had struck burst into fresh flames. Everyone in the mall was running in mad chaos. There was no place to take cover. There was no shelter to escape. Bodies ran screaming on fire. One by one the citizens of the mall burst into flames. Shelby ran in vain, but there was no escaping the inferno. The stretch of the mall kept repeating itself in a cycle, like a treadmill. She sprinted as fast as she could, evading the falling plates and bodies ablaze until she gave up from exhaustion and discovered that there was one building left intact, and that was her very own Pete's Diner. She walked into the safe haven in relief. Shockingly, everything was normal inside; breakfast was being served as usual, all the seats in the house were filled with happy and eager customers. A waiter tossed her an apron and told her to get back to work. She went to her first table and there was Lucy. "May I have two smiley face pancakes?" she asked sweetly. Shelby was too traumatized to respond. "May I have the Pancakes?" she asked again sweetly. Again, Shelby was too dumb and transfixed to answer. "May I have the pancakes?" she repeated again more abrasively. "The pancakes! I need the Pancakes!" she screamed, her voice suddenly demonic. Shelby was shaken by its deep and diabolic tone into awareness. As she looked down, she saw that where Lucy's eyeballs had once been, two cherries now took their place in their sockets. Shelby gasped in terror. "THE PANCAKES! THE PANCAKES!" She demanded, her cherry eyes convulsing in malevolent rage. "GIVE ME THE PANCAKES!" she screamed so loud and fearsome that the cherries squirted, emitting the molasses goo-like blood all over the table. "Wake up," she demanded. "What?" Shelby asked bewildered. "Wake up," Lucy repeated.

***

"Wake up!" Todd had a cold cloth pressed to her cheek. "Wake up!" the waiter gently commanded.

At the sound of his voice, Shelby slowly regained consciousness. When her eyes focused she saw that there was a mass of people crowding around her.

"The ambulance is on their way. Can you tell me where your parents are? Did they come here with you?"

"Huh?" Shelby was still unaware of everything that was going on. "What? Why would my parents come with me to my job?"

Todd didn't find her incoherence a good sign.

"Do you know their number so I can call them?"

"Why do you need to call them?" She was utterly confused. She knew she had fainted. She felt sweaty and damp. She wiped her brow with her hand again, but this time felt a set of caterpillar eyebrows.

A BALLOON AT NOON

Colin W. Campbell

Way out in the wet monsoon

a spaceship came down at noon.

But that's the day

when folks just say

it's only a weather balloon.

Impossible Tower Remodeled - Denny Marshall

Playing With Worms

Denny E. Marshall

William and Janet stroll the park on a nice evening. Suddenly a tornado touches down and is coming at them. Both are swept into the funnel. Forty minutes later, they land. They look around to see where they are. The three moons in the sky a give-a-way it is not earth.

Amanda and Nick adjust the dials until they reach the desired settings. Then Mr. Clark walks into the room. He yells at them, 'I have told you before not to play with my rock and mineral specimen wormhole vacuum." They run off, Mr. Clark laughs. Kids will be kids.

Do I Know You?

By Maddie McLeod

A draft of wind catches the fraying ends of my faded pink cardigan, sending a wave of shivers crashing over my body. The dim lamp on the corner of the street flickers again, as if it's trying to remind me that coming here so late at night was a bad idea.

I don't need a reminder.

Looking across the street, I stare dully at the closed local grocery store. My eyes then wander to the abandoned car maintenance garage before finally settling on the run down brick–and–mortar bank.

When my family and I first moved here, I wasn't a fan of the whole small–town idea (and as I later learned, Granisle wasn't even a town; it was a village). Suddenly, everyone knew my name, just like how I knew the names of everyone around me. Here, I couldn't pretend to be something else because someone, sooner or later, would find out the truth. My life became entwined with other people's lives either because of choice or because of force.

Honestly, I'm still not sure how I feel about that.

A snapping branch immediately tears me away from my idle musings and back to my dark and eerie surroundings. I look to my right and see a man walking towards me. The street lamp is casting long, sunken shadows across his features, smearing his eyes into a nature–made mask. I tug my cardigan tighter around me.

"I was starting to think that you weren't coming," I say as Sawyer stops in front of me. He keeps his distance, though, roughly an arm's length away. His shoulders look tense against the cold early spring air.

Sawyer tilts his head to the side slightly. His words come out tersely. "I was taking my time because I thought you wouldn't want to come."

"I promised you I would come. So here I am, standing here by myself at midnight. I could get kidnapped, you know." I send him a tiny smile in my attempt to lighten the atmosphere.

He looks like he's in pain, I think to myself as Sawyer gives me a tight smile in return.

"So what was so important that I had to meet you here?"

"I need to tell you something, Phoenix. It's extremely important."

I raise my eyebrows. "What's wrong?"

"Nothing's wrong," Sawyer says defensively. "I just need you to answer something."

A quiet and tiny laugh presses its way through my lips. I smile again at Sawyer, trying to look reassuring. He lifts his face slightly so that the ugly mask of the night disappears for a moment. I lock my eyes with his green ones. "What is it?"

"Do you trust me?"

I sputter. "You're kidding, right? You know I do."

"But do you *really* trust me?" Sawyer emphasizes, suddenly reaching his arm out and resting his hand on my shoulder. "I need to know if you trust me one–hundred percent."

"Why?" I laugh nervously. "Did you do something bad?"

Maybe he did, I think as his jaw clenches. Sawyer drops his hand back down to his side as I carefully take a step back.

"Sometime soon, I might be. But that's why I need to know if you can trust me."

"What's going on, Sawyer? What's happening?"

"I'll tell you later," he says, dismissing my question with his hand. "Can you just answer my question?" I can't help but notice that his voice rises slightly, ringing past my ears and into the silent night.

"You can just tell me—"

"Phoenix!" he shouts. This time, both of his hands land on my shoulders. I cringe beneath his strong grasp as a surprised gasp escapes from within me.

Then Sawyer immediately lets go of me, stepping back and running his right hand through his dusty blonde hair.

"I didn't mean—"

"No," I interrupt, trying to shake off what just happened. "I kept pushing when I shouldn't have. I'm sorry. As for your question, yes. Yes, I do trust you completely." I quickly cover the few steps between us and wrap my arms around his waist. Then I snuggle my head further into his chest as Sawyer places his strong arm around me, laying his head down on top of mine.

"No matter what you've done or what's happening, I will still trust you, Sawyer Jones. I—Sawyer?"

He lets go of me as I straighten up, rubbing the point of my neck where I just felt a prick. I look down at his hand and see a needle, dripping slowly with a clear liquid.

"Sawyer?" I ask again as my vision starts to fade in and back out. Two Sawyers are now standing in front of me.

"What did you do?" I scream, my body feeling sluggish. My blurred eyes spot the asphalt. I feel the sudden urge to lie down. But instead, I glare at Sawyer as I stumble backwards.

"You said you trust me," he simply replies, calmly standing there.

"That was before the needle!" I yell, dropping to my knees. A searing pain begins to build up right where the needle had punctured my skin. It feels like it's racing up towards my brain.

"I know what I'm doing, Phoenix."

I clench my jaw, raising my hands up to my burning skull. "Oh, really? And what's that? Kill me?"

"No," Sawyer whispers softly. "Why else would I tell you to meet me alone and at midnight?"

My body doubles over as the realization hits me. But it's impossible. This is Sawyer. He wouldn't... he couldn't do such a thing, could he?

Right before I pass out, my ears manage to hear Sawyer confirm what I had been dreading.

"I'm kidnapping you, Phoenix."

The End.

"See but don't
be seen?
Leave no footprints?
Ha!"

Footprints – Jay Duret

Mister Frog-A-Misery and Me

John W Sexton

In the pond in my back garden

there lives a frog-skinned man.

He survives on grass and soggy weeds

and drinks from the watering can.

Mister Frog-a-Misery

is the name I give to him

because he mopes about the place

in his baggy leathery skin.

But though he looks a misery-guts

he's a prankster to his bones

and between us we're the tricksters

on all the village homes.

We're the ones who painted

all your windows black

and stole socks from the washing line

and never brought them back.

Of course, it's only me

who gets the blame for all these minor crimes

for Mister Frog-a-Misery

slips away each time.

The Hypnotist Chameleon
By Sephonē Zorro

Chameleon lived in Madagascar, where he loved nothing
more than to eat big, juicy katydids. He would spend hours....
slowly....slowly....slowly....creeping along a tree branch to get
within two feet of one, then....**Z-A-P!**—out would strike his
sticky tongue like a lightning bolt to grab the surprised insect
and pop it into his mouth. Chameleon would then be so happy
that his skin would flash from tree-leaf green to such patterns of
yellow, black and red that he looked like a Persian rug.

But then it was time to start all over again, stalking his next
tidbit. As he stalked so slowly, it took most of the day to catch
enough insects of any kind for a decent lunch. He really wanted
to spend more time basking in the sun. There had to be an
easier, quicker way to get his food.

And....*humm*....Yes, yes there was, he thought, and smiled
to his smart, tricky old self. Time to go hang out with those
lemur kids.

Unlike Chameleon, the lemur kids were fast and wild, but
like him they also loved to eat katydids. Indeed, when
Chameleon spotted him, there was Lester Lemur sitting high on
a limb examining a big, fat katydid. Lemurs like to play with
their food before eating it.

"Hello, Lester," Chameleon said. "Have you ever been hypnotized?"

"I don't think so," said Lester. "What is that?"

"Oh it's great fun," said Chameleon. "Let me show you. Now, look into my eyes, Lester. **Look into my eyes!"**

When Lester did, the sly lizard slowly moved his eyes. Each one drifted out, then one rolled clockwise and the other counterclockwise. Lester's own eyes tried to follow, but couldn't. They darted back and forth so fast and in such weird ways that Lester became dizzy. He started to sway on the branch and he felt sick at his stomach. Just before he fell out of the tree....***Z-A-P!*** out struck Chameleon's tongue and grabbed the katydid right out of Lester's hand.

"Hey! *Ouch!* What the...." Lester hit the ground with a thump.

"Pretty powerful, my hypnosis, no?" grinned Chameleon.

"Hey, give me back my katydid!" yelled Lester.

"What katydid?" said Chameleon, munching and crunching the insect in his mouth. "In my hypnotic spell you just thought you had a katydid.

"I'll prove it to you," Chameleon continued. "Next time you are sure you have a katydid, come and find me. I'll hypnotize you again, and the same thing will happen. You'll soon see you really didn't have a katydid. Tell your brothers and other lemur friends, too. I'm sure they'll find my hypnosis just as amazing."

Lester was no dope. He knew exactly what this wise-guy Chameleon had done. But Chameleon was so pleased with himself....and let's face it, he only has a lizard brain.... and he was just sure he'd fooled the young primate. Lester decided to play along, and get his revenge.

"Oh, wow, Mr. Chameleon, sir, you are right! How amazing that this hypnosis thing can make you think things that are not. Why I must have just thought I had a katydid, just like I thought I was sitting high in a tree, and now find I'm really on the ground, and with a big lump on my head. Powerful stuff, your hypnosis, Mr. Chameleon. Will you teach me how to do hypnosis, too?"

Chameleon thought for a moment.

"Well, it takes a lot of time to learn, and I don't give lessons for free," he said.

"Of course not," said Lester Lemur. "But I'll work hard, and I hope you'll accept many nice fat katydids, like the one I thought I had just a minute ago, as payment to teach me."

"Yes, yes," said Chameleon, as his skin turned to a red and yellow checkerboard pattern in happy anticipation of a feast. "Yes, I think that will do. You can be my student for all the years it will take to make you a truly expert hypnotist."

"Great!" said Lester. "Wait right here. I'll go catch a katydid, and we can start right away."

Soon Lester was back with a fat, struggling katydid, at least three inches long. Chameleon licked both his eyes—which stick out from his face like two ping-pong balls with big knobs in the centers—and even licked the back of his head, he was so excited.

"Now let me try first," said Lester. "I know I won't get it right, and then you can show me how to really do it, and make this katydid I only think I have now disappear."

"Ok," said Chameleon, more than willing to humor his victim.

"Look into my eyes!" commanded the lemur.

The lizard did as he was told, but when he did, Lester crossed his eyes. The big knobs on Chameleon's eyes over where his pupils sit rotated so far inward that they both got stuck under the bony plates in the middle of his face.

"Hey!" hissed Chameleon. "My eyes are stuck! I can't see!" He swayed back and forth and shook his head, but could not get the knobs on his eyes out from under the bony plate on either side of his nose.

"Wow!" said Lester. "Can you see the katydid?"

"No, I cannot. And I think I'm going to fall."

"What a wonderful teacher you are! I learned hypnosis on the very first try!" said Lester Lemur as he munched and crunched on the insect as loudly as he could.

Chameleon fell from the tree and landed head-first in a big pile of muddy leaves.

"Help, me! Help me, Lester, please! I can't see."

Lester climbed down from the tree and pulled Chameleon out of the mud by his tail.

"Ok. But this hypnosis thing seems way too dangerous. I'll fix your eyes only on condition that neither of us will try it ever again. Promise?"

Chameleon knew he'd been had, but he really needed Lester's help.

"I promise," he said.

Lester used his thumb and forefinger to push hard onto the lizard's two eyes, freeing them from the bony trap as he rotated them out to the side. *P-O-P!*

"Ouch!" hissed Chameleon, but now he could see again.

"Here you go, Sport," said Lester. "You've been such a good little patient that the doctor here is giving you a treat." He then stuffed a big, nasty leaf into Chameleon's mouth.

"Tasty, isn't it? Imagine, just a minute ago you thought this was some big, fat, yucky insect."

Humbled, Chameleon chewed on the nasty, bitter leaf. He wanted to be sure he would always remember what happened that day, and never, ever mess with a lemur again.

(END)

TEN HOPI KACHINA

By Matthew J. Barbour

Ten Hopi kachina marching in a line, one climbs into the kiva –

then there are…

Nine Hopi kachina mouths all agape, one eats some piki bread –

then there are…

Eight Hopi kachina calling rain down from heaven, one sees an awanyu –

then there are…

Seven Hopi kachina collecting prayer sticks, one plays the flute –

then there are…

Six Hopi kachina dance and sing and jive, one stops to fight an ogre –

then there are…

Five Hopi kachina knocking at the door, one comes inside the pueblo —

then there are...

Four Hopi kachina staring straight at me, one scares a little child —

then there are...

Three Hopi kachina cooking chili stew, one goes to get some posole —

then there are...

Two Hopi kachina arms stretched to the sun, one grabs a scarlet macaw —

then there is just...

One Hopi kachina standing atop the mesa high, he gathers all the others —

then ascends into the sky.

END

"It's all good."

Good – Jay Duret

My Story is Better

By Monica Adrian

Scene - Two young girls camping outside in their backyard in a tent.

Hailey and Jordan are 9-years-old.

HAILEY- Let's tell stories.

JORDAN - Okay but they have to scary.

HAILEY - Duh.

JORDAN - Okay, I go first. Once upon a time there was Hailey and there was Jordan. Every time they got together they kept getting in a fight. This kept happening again and again. Then this one night the parents decided to make them have a sleepover so they'd get along. So at the sleepover a doll popped out!! D O L a doll!!! And then it was a like a zombie—

HAILEY - My turn!! There were best friends named Jordan and Hailey. They got into a big fight at school. A food fight, no, I'm kidding. Then what happened was there's this doll that hmmmm... I don't like dolls. So there's this doll that I owned that I looked at, not looked at—it was just in my room. Then we had a sleepover and the doll became a zombie, and then the zombie doll started walking towards us like "huuuuuhhhh," and then what happened was we started to hug each other, and then the zombie doll flew back to the shelf and became unalive. The end.

JORDAN - That was just like my story!!

HAILEY - No, my story was better.

JORDAN - But you took all my ideas!

HAILEY - Fine. This time I'll go first. Once upon a time there was Jordan and Hailey. Now, they were both scared of clowns so what happened was, there was a clown at the mall when they were going into Claire's. No not Claire's, sorry, uh, let me think of a store in there. Pretzel, yeah the pretzel place. Then they saw this clown by a tree, so they both went into the pretzel place and then the clown was like, "huuuuuhhhh." So then the clown jumped on the roof. The clown flew way up high into the sky like a shooting rocket. The end. And they were never scared of clowns again. The end.

JORDAN - That wasn't even scary. And why does the clown sound just like the doll from the other story?

HAILEY - I don't know, okay? It just does.

JORDAN - Whatever. My turn! There was a clown who lived in this place in, um—he liked to scare kids. Uh, wait. No, he didn't like to scare kids, he liked to scare everybody on the earth. This kid came up to this, no and a parent. The parent said, "Hi," and the clown said "cgcgcgcgcgcggc." He meant to say, "I need sunscreen. Can you buy me some sunscreen?" And then the parent said, "Okay, well no thank you. You are too creepy for my child."

HAILEY - What the heck, Jordan?

JORDAN - I wasn't finished yet.

HAILEY - Why would the clown want sunscreen? That's so random.

JORDAN - Clowns are really white, okayyy? They need sunscreen.

HAILEY - They're white because they have makeup on.

JORDAN - No they have white skin. That's why they're scary. And then they put a bunch of makeup over it to make themselves scarier.

HAILEY - Yes, they put makeup on but that includes the white part.

JORDAN - Then why are their hands white too?

HAILEY - They put makeup on those as well.

JORDAN - Who puts makeup on their hands?

HAILEY - Clowns do. Wait, no. Don't they wear gloves? They wear gloves, Jordan. They don't even have white hands.

JORDAN - Yes huh.

HAILEY - Nuh—uh.

JORDAN - Let me just finish my story. Where was I? Oh yeah. So the parent was like, "You are too weird for my child." Then the clown got mad and gobbled them up. The end.

HAILEY - Whaat? How could a clown just gobble them up? They're people, not monsters.

JORDAN - They're monster people.

HAILEY - No, they're just creepy people.

JORDAN - Then how do they have giant feet?

HAILEY - They don't. They just wear giant shoes.

JORDAN - That's stupid. Why would anyone wear shoes that don't fit?

HAILEY - I don't know. It's a clown thing.

JORDAN - Okay, I have a new story.

HAILEY - It's not your turn.

JORDAN - Once upon a time there were two friends Hailey and Jordan at a sleepover. They got into a fight because Hailey wouldn't like any of Jordan's stories and thought hers were so much better.

HAILEY - No. Mine just make sense.

JORDAN - How does a clown flying into the sky like a rocket make any sense?

HAILEY - Well, the clown had a jetpack.

JORDAN - What kind of clown has a jetpack?

HAILEY - I don't know. It's a clown thing.

JORDAN - It is not!

HAILEY - Is too!

JORDAN - You just won't admit that your stories don't make any sense either!

(Mom peeks head into the tent)

45

MOM - What are you girls bickering about? I can hear you from the house.

HAILEY - Jordan thinks clowns are real monsters.

MOM - Is that what you're fighting about?

JORDAN - Mom, she keeps interrupting all my stories.

MOM - Is that true, Hailey?

HAILEY - I'm only interrupting because I don't understand them.

MOM - How about this? I'll tell you a story.

(Mom sits in tent)

MOM - Once upon a time there were two girls named Emily and Karen.

HAILEY - No, they have to be named Hailey and Jordan.

MOM - It's not nice to interrupt Hailey.

JORDAN - They have to be named Hailey and Jordan.

MOM - Fine. Once upon a time there were two girls named Hailey and Jordan. They lived in a magical kingdom.

HAILEY - No, it has to be a scary story.

MOM - A magical kingdom with werewolves. **(pause)** On every full moon the princess was not allowed to go outside.

They locked her up in a tower. So one full moon she heard the howling of the werewolves. She loved the sound of the howling so she decided to howl with them.

JORDAN - Was she a werewolf too?

MOM - I'm getting there. **(pause)** The princess didn't know that she was part werewolf. That's why she was able to smell so well.

HAILEY - I bet she turns into a werewolf.

MOM - Yes, the princess's scent could—

JORDAN - I bet she's a werewolf too.

HAILEY - That's what I said.

JORDAN - Well I said it first.

HAILEY - You're just copying me.

MOM - And then she turned into a werewolf. The end. Happy?

JORDAN - Hey, we weren't even in the story.

MOM - Well, you two weren't being good listeners so I decided to end there.

HAILEY - No, finish the story.

MOM - Nope. The end. Go to bed.

Star

By Peter MacQuarrie

Starlight,

star bright,

you are shining

so bright.

I stand under

the sky

watching you

at night.

Starlight,

star bright,

you are shining

so bright.

You are

an amazing

and wonderful

sight.

Starlight,

star bright,

you are shining

so bright.

Sneaky Swimboticus

By Art Bupkis

There appeared a new toy named "Sneaky Swimboticus",

Who was placed by the tub with a frog, and a duck, and a pink hippopotamus.

There he just sat for most that first day,

'til Mother drew water, and he spotted his prey.

Hiding down deep, beneath Billy's hand,

He watched as it splashed and kept trying to stand.

Mother was having most terrible troubles

Trying to keep the brat thing in the bubbles.

Then swift but quiet, around Billy's left leg,

Sneaky kicked with his flippers, and headed for Meg.

She squealed as his trident rammed her wet butt.

Mother screamed *"**Billy!**"* He answered her, *"**What?!**"*

So Mother took Sneaky Swimboticus's batteries away,

"Ruining!" cried Billy, the gift Grandmother'd just sent for his birthday.

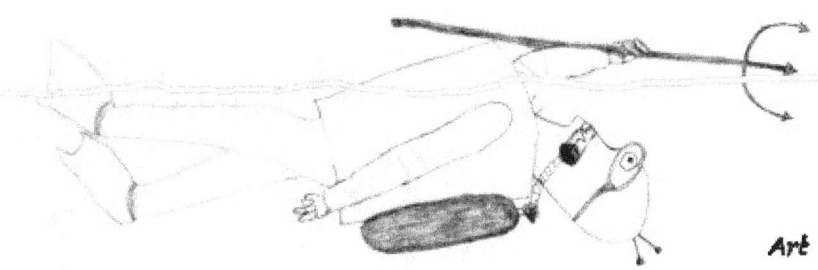

Meg's Revenge

Bad old Botty,

In the potty.

Joan of Arc - Kyle Hemmings

A Peculiar Thing

Scáth Beorh

How Therese found the Kingdom,

a peculiar thing—

She likes to dry clothes on the line.

She cries, "Every bell has the prettiest ring!"

She loves bread unleavened, new wine.

She jumps when her pup romps to nuzzle and paw.

She flits when her kitten claws trees.

She once raved as she bathed at the seashore and saw

a bevy of bumbling bees

who (said Therese) had cute little knees.

Unbalanced Party: It's a Trap

By Lee Newman

"You're sure this will work," the tall handsome paladin asked, leaning far over the hunched dwarf's shoulder. "It's just that last time-"

"I know what happened last time, ye soddin' git!"

Enraged spittle flew from the dwarf's mouth, spattering droplets onto his long red beard and flecking the paladin's face and flowing golden hair. "Now let me work an' shut yer flappin' gob! Concentration is key! It's a rogue's most important skill!"

"Actually, that's wrong. It's dexterity," condescended a voice from behind a stone pillar roughly twenty feet away. A sorcerer with cropped brown hair poked his hooded head out from cover. "Concentration is far more important to those who practice the magical arts." He paused.

"Also, I'd like to coalesce with Daveth on recounting the failure of your last attempt to even detect a trap, let alone disarm one."

"Uh, Mordwin, maybe we should just let Wulf, concentrate," Daveth, the paladin, cautioned.

Mordwin, having been born and raised in the company of other magi in a secluded yet prestigious academy of sorcerers, lacked certain social skills needed to interact with those outside of his societal circles. Namely, he lacked all of them. Daveth had saved Mordwin from the business end of Betty, the massive battle axe of Bofric Redwulf, affectionately known as "Wulf", on more than one occasion since the three had joined company. Wulf bristled, "Mordwin, ye pointy nosed, gabblin' gobbed, robe wearin', spell slingin', know it all. If ye don't shut that mewling maw of yers while my deft hands do their work, I swear to the stone I'll drop ye faster than a bawdy barmaids panties after twenty tankards!" Mordwin slunk back behind the pillar. "I think you meant 'daft' hands...although I do appreciate the trouble you must have gone through to add alliteration to some of those insults," he said.

"Just let him work, Mordwin," said Daveth harshly. "He knows what he's doing this time. You know what you're doing this time. Right, Wulf?"

"Th-This time?" Wulf fumed angrily before settling. "Aye...Aye this time, more or less I do. Now shut it!"

"More or less?" asked Mordwin.

"Shut it!" Wulf screamed.

The unlikely companions had spent hours navigating this dungeon. Days following leads to find it. Weeks penniless and even longer listening to Wulf suggest over and over that they eat Mordwin's mare, Gwendolyn. Wulf inhaled deeply as he eased his first lock pick into the keyhole of the large chest. A heavy bead of sweat rolled down the dwarf's furrowed brow. He exhaled. "So far so good," he whispered. He slipped in a second pick and began to turn. "Easy...easy," he coaxed the lock. "Come on, lass. Open sesam—" There was a loud click. "Uh oh."

"Uh oh?! What do you mean 'Uh oh'? That was an 'uh oh' click?" Mordwin called in a panic, still hiding behind the column.

"Was that an 'uh oh' click, Wulf," asked Daveth. "On a scale from one to—"

"Shut it and run!" Wulf yelled, bolting out of the room and slamming a heavy oak door behind him. Daveth and Mordwin ran to the door, but found Wulf had barred it behind him.

"Scoundrel!" cursed Mordwin.

"Uh...Wulf! Wulf! You left us in here! Wulf!" Daveth and Mordwin hammered on the door with their fists.

"I knew we couldn't trust him, Daveth!" Mordwin cried, his eyes welling up. "I told you there was no such thing as a competent dwarven rogue! And, he's filthy! All that belching and gas! Curse that filthy little—" Mordwin gave a rather effeminate howl of exasperation and returned to pounding on the door. "And, now we're doomed! DOOM—"

They heard the bar on the opposite side of the door slide free. The door opened to reveal a beaming Bofric Redwulf on the other side.

"Ye shoulda seen yer faces. Scared as a buncha wee pups. I may be a rogue—"

"To be determined." Mordwin chimed in, trying to compose himself under the guise of brushing off his robes.

"I may be a rogue," Wulf continued, glaring at Mordwin, "but I'm nay a turncoat. I just wanted ta teach ye nay sayers a lesson. The chest is open. The lock wasn't even booby–trapped." Wulf strode past his fellows triumphantly.

"See?" He flung the lid open, not noticing a thin chain leading from one of its corners to the floor. The chain went taught, slamming the lid back down. There was a very loud click from the floor.

"Uh...Ah...okay. That might have been a trap. I only checked the lock. I dinna think ta check around the chest."

"Just grab the chest and let's go!" Mordwin screeched in terror.

"We canna! It's bolted ta the ground, ya nit!" Wulf replied in a panic.

"Do you guys smell something?" Daveth asked.

"I canna help it! It happens when I get panicky! I have a nervous colon!" said Wulf defensively.

"No, not that! Look!" Daveth pointed to a thick green gas hissing from grates in the floor. Mordwin ran for the door.

"Locked! Just great. I die starving and asphyxiated by poison gas next to a paladin who I have yet to see do anything remotely good and a dwarf who thinks he's a thief, " Mordwin whimpered." Rogue, ye goat faced nancy! And I am one! Just blow up the door with yer magics and whatnots!"

"Are you insane? We have no idea what kind of gas this is. It could be flammable. I could blow us all to kingdom come."

Wulf snatched the staff from Mordwin's hand and pointed it at the door. "Oh Hells! Give it here! How does this blasted twig work?"

"No!" Mordwin and Daveth yelled in unison, finally in agreement about something.

"What was that silly fireball spell Mordwin always used to light the campfire?" Wulf thought quickly. A huge determined grin exploded on his face as he remembered. Wulf leveled the head of the staff at the door. Again, Mordwin and Daveth screamed in protest, dashing to close the space between them, but it was too late. Wulf bellowed, "Ignatious Expelarum!" A ball of fire plumed from the staff and shot at the door.

Down the silent hall, a large black rat lifted its head from foraging to look toward the closed door where the three men had entered. Smoke began to billow from beneath the door. The rat sniffed inquisitively. Suddenly the massive door was sent rocketing from its hinges past the rat, tailed by a cloud of smoke and flame. The terrified, and now slightly singed rat, retreated into a nearby hole. There, in the empty doorway, stood Wulf, his beard completely singed off, his naked face soot covered.

"See?" he coughed, a small black wisp of smoke exiting his mouth. "I told ye it'd work."

Daveth emerged from behind the monstrous chest and let out a sigh. Opening the chest, he reached in to retrieve a small gold leafed box.

"Okay, let's move out," Daveth said. Mordwin peaked over the open lid of the chest cautiously. He stood and collected himself, straightening his robes. He walked by a still stunned Wulf and snatched his staff back, exiting the room. He returned a moment later, poking his head back in at the beardless blackened dwarf.

"Just so you know," he said, "this doesn't make you a mage too." Wulf nodded slowly, his stare still blank, and reached up to extinguish a single smoldering bristle from his chin.

Authors, Poets, and Illustrators

Monica Adrian is an artist and writer born on Halloween. She graduated from CSUN with a Bachelors degree in English/Creative Writing.

Matthew J. Barbour is a speculative fiction author living with his wife and three children in Bernalillo, New Mexico. When he is not writing fiction, Mr. Barbour manages Jemez Historic Site and contributes to a number of regional newspapers, including the *Red Rocks Reporter* and the *Sandoval Signpost*.

Scáth Beorh is the author of the story collections *Children & Other Wicked Things* (JWK Fiction), *Always After Thieves Watch* (Wildside Press), and the MG novel *October House* (Emby Press, Oct 2014) as well as the forthcoming epistolary novel *Blood* (Emby, 2015). He lives with his wife Ember in a Folk Victorian carriage house on the Atlantic Coast.

The Rev Dr. Art Bupkis—poet, comic, philosopher, and international man of letters—is the unnatural twin brother of Ms. Sephonē Zorro, whose work has appeared several times previously in **Stinkwaves Magazine**. As is Ms. Zorro, Art is a literary ward of L. R. Baxter

Colin W. Campbell writes short fiction and poetry in Sarawak on the lovely green island of Borneo and faraway in Yunnan in southwest China: www.colincampbell.org

Authors, Poets, and Illustrators

Lela Marie De La Garza has had work published in *Creepy Gnome*, *Passion Beyond Words*, *Black Denim*, *Yellow Mama*, *Bewildering Stories*, and *The Western Online*. Her latest novel, *Mistral*, was published in December of 2014. She was born in Denver, CO. in 1943 while her father was serving in WWII. She currently resides in San Antonio, TX with three and a half cats and a visiting raccoon.

Kyle Hemmings lives and works in New Jersey. He has been published in *Your Impossible Voice*, *Night Train*, *Toad*, *Matchbox and* elsewhere. His latest chapbooks are *Underground Chrysanthemums* from Red Bird Press and *Terminal* from White Knuckle Press. He loves 50s Sci-Fi movies, manga comics, and pre-punk garage bands of the 60s. He blogs at
http://upatberggasse19.blogspot.com/

Although **Denny E. Marshall** has no art education or training, he enjoys drawing by hand and computer. Recent credits include cover art for *Perihelion SF* & *Dreams & Nightmares 94*, and featured poet in *Scifaikuest #39*. Denny does not have a Facebook page or Twitter account but does have a website with previously published works, http://dennymarshall.com/

Jay Duret is a San Francisco based writer and illustrator who blogs at www.jayduret.com. More than two dozen of Jay's stories have been published or are forthcoming in online and print journals, including *Narrative Magazine*, *Blue Fifth Review*, *Gargoyle* and *December*. Jay's first novel, *Nine Digits*, tells the story of 15 year-old Nee-Nee Marcus' quest to win $100 million on a reality TV contest. See the book trailer at www.ninedigits.com. Jay's illustrations are posted daily to Instagram @joefaces and twitter @jayduret.

Authors, Poets, and Illustrators cont.

While finishing up her high school education, 17 year old **Maddie McLeod** loves to craft short stories that leave her readers craving more. She has been previously published in Canvas Lit. Magazine as well as Cuckoo Quarterly. She is also extremely grateful that Stinkwaves Magazine decided to take on her story.

Laurie Meyers is a children's writer living part-time in New Jersey and part-time in the fantasy worlds she builds in her head. She once had 12 pet mice, which was somewhere between too many and not enough. She is a member of SCBWI and blogs at www.laurimeyers.com.

Lee Newman is a South Carolina resident and USC graduate. Lee enjoys horror, graphic novels, humor, literature, film, and any amalgamation in between. He enjoys writing everything from children's books, to short horror, to romantic comedy. http://facebook.com/ravenwritindesk https://quarterreads.com/

Peter McQuarrie is an enigma. He lives in a darkling forest of Mendocino County, California. Visit him at www.petermacquarrie.com.

John W. Sexton lives in the Republic of Ireland and is the author of five poetry collections, the most recent being *The Offspring of the Moon* (Salmon Poetry in 2013). He has also written two YA novels which have been published by the O'Brien Press, *The Johnny Coffin Diaries* and *Johnny Coffin School-Dazed*, both of which have been translated into both Italian and Serbian. In 2007 he was awarded a Patrick and Katherine Kavanagh Fellowship in Poetry.

Sephonē Zorro is the author of many fairy tales, myths, children's stories, and poems. Along with her twin, the comic and social satirist, The Rt. Rev. Dr. Art Bupkis, she is a literary ward of L.R. Baxter.

THaNK YoU'S

As always, we want to thank our very talented contributors for another great issue. Without them there would be no Stinkwaves. If you would like to be a part of our accomplished crew, visit www.stinkwavesmagazine.com for submission guidelines, or email us at submissions@stinkwavesmagazine.com with any questions.

Follow us on Facebook and Twitter to stay up to date on the latest Stinkwaves shenanigans.

If you enjoyed this issue of Stinkwaves, go to www.handersenpublishing.com to discover more enjoyable books available thru Handersen Publishing.

Handersen Publishing